To Florence . . . .

Here are pages of
    laughter to make
moments merrier.

Love,
Sharlene
   &
Jim

Kid Stuff

KID STUFF

Stories About the Funny and

Touching Things Kids Say and Do

Selected by Jan Miller

Illustrated by John Overmyer

HALLMARK EDITIONS

CONTENTS

My four-year-old Janie was underfoot all morning. Finally I said to her, "Honey, please—why don't you go over and see how old Mrs. Connors is?"

Janie went, but was back within half a minute. "Mommy," she said, "Mrs. Connors said it's none of your business how old she is!"

Agatha D. Brungardt

When my brother completed a merit badge project for Boy Scouts, he immediately showed his work throughout the neighborhood. My parents were mortified to find that the project, a box of assorted, horrendous insects, was labeled: "Bugs Found In and About My Home."

Dorothy G. Dreher

My husband and I couldn't help laughing when our four-year-old daughter told us about a little boy who had chased her around a table trying to kiss her. Upset by the laughter, she insisted that we stop. We tried, but continued to smile as we thought about the incident.

"Mother—I asked you to stop laughing," our daughter said.

"Darling, we're not laughing," I explained.

"Well," she replied unhappily, "but your teeth still are!"

Retta Duckworth

Looking through my son's trousers before tossing them into the washer, I came across a soiled, much-handled note. It read: "Puff, puff, draw in, draw in, puff, puff." I quickly checked my cigarette supply, then checked my son.

"What," I asked, "is your explanation of these instructions?"

"Oh, I've been looking for that," he answered. "I'm learning the Star Spangled Banner on the harmonica!"

Mrs. Arthur Putman

While my husband was out of town attending a medical convention, I told our four-year-old son that he would have to be the "man of the house." He immediately sat down in his father's big reclining chair and solemnly announced, "Okay, I'm listening." *Clarys E. Sheiban*

A family who had just moved into a new neighborhood was anxious to make a good impression. But the neighbors seemed cold and made no overtures of welcome. The mother of the brood was overjoyed when finally her youngest son ran in and announced happily, "Mommy, the lady down the street asked my name today!"

"Oh, how nice!" exclaimed the mother enthusiastically. "And then what did she do?"

"Then she gave it to the policeman," the boy said. *Quoted in* FAMILY WEEKLY

My husband and two sons were walking in the downtown section of our city when 12-year-old Chris paused to survey several photographs in the window of a nightclub. The pictures,

quite naturally, were of somewhat scantily at-
tired girls. My husband commented good-
naturedly, "I thought you didn't like girls,
Chris."

"I don't, but I want to see what I'm miss-
ing," he mused.   *Jean Bonner*

Like all mothers, I was worn out after a rainy
day that kept my three children in the house. I
decided to go to my room, and asked the children not to disturb me.

"Why, Mommie?" questioned my youngest.

"Because I'm verging on a nervous break-
down!" Just as I slammed the bedroom door,
in walked my husband, home from work and
unaware of my mood.

"What's going on here, kids?" he asked the
children.

Replied the eight-year-old: "Mommy just
verged."   *Jean Bonner*

One evening my four-year-old sister, Cindy,
came in to show her father how she looked in a
new dress.

"My," he said, trying to look impressed,
"you're really growing like a weed."

Cindy scowled, replying, "No, Daddy—not
like a weed. Like a flower!"   *Jan Miller*

Insisting that our dog gets more attention from our three daughters than he does, my husband one evening complained, "Sometimes I think you girls care more about that pooch than you do me."

"That's not so, Daddy," our five-year-old solemnly replied. "We love you both the same."

Mrs. Robert Hending

While vacationing in the state of Washington, I took my family to Mass on Sunday in a small town parish church. We were lucky enough to get seats, but later arrivals had to stand. Among them I noticed several grandmotherly-looking women with children. As I got up to offer my seat, I asked our nine-year-old son to do the same. To my surprise, he walked over to a cute little girl about seven years old and grandly motioned her to his seat.

What could I do but beam my approval?

Michael R. Rector

Little Gay got very restless during the Mass. "The priest prays too long," she said afterwards.

A few weeks later, Father came for dinner and I asked him to say grace before the meal.

After he had offered a brief blessing, Gay looked at him and said, "You don't pray so long when you're hungry."   *Anne Dirkman*

SCHOOL DAZE

To stimulate her young pupils, a first-grade teacher arranged to take her class on an "educational tour" of a farmyard. But one small boy saw right through her scheme. "Don't look, don't look!" he warned his buddy. "If we look we'll have to tell about it tomorrow!"

Quoted in NEWBURGH-BEACON NEWS

A young teacher I know was to be married at the end of the school year. As class was dismissed one day, a shy Mexican-American girl placed a package and a letter on the teacher's desk, then went swiftly out of the room. Left alone, the teacher opened the letter.

"Dear, sweet Senorita Brown," she read. "We are all so sorry that you are going to leave us, but we want you to be happy. I have been saving and saving to buy you a beautiful present for your wedding, but all I could save is $1.62 and I can't get a very nice present for so little.

"Mama told me that when people get married they have all new things, so they don't have any rags. Yet they will need rags to scrub the bath, and to dust the furniture, and to wash the windows. So Mama collected some of our rags, she does not need them all, and she even gave me two of the baby's diapers. I hope you will like my gift. With much love, Conchita."

Through a mist of tears the teacher opened the package. In it were soft old cloths of many colors, torn neatly into squares, and all carefully washed and ironed—two dozen of them, including the two diapers.   *Harriet H. Jones*

There's nothing like a little girl to greet you after a long hard day at the office, reports a man whose daughter just entered second grade. The moppet met him at the door with a hug and a kiss and the comforting words, "Guess who threw up at school today, Daddy?"

Quoted in GRAND RAPIDS PRESS

Our next-door neighbor, whose wife had suddenly become ill and had to be hospitalized, found himself with the full responsibility of caring for their five children. The first morning he rushed around in a panic, trying to see that each child was ready for school on time. Then he hurried all of them out the door. A few seconds later, the youngest boy returned. His father shoved him out the door again, warning that if he didn't run all the way he'd never make it. A few more seconds lapsed, then a timid voice at the door said, "But, Daddy, I don't go to school yet!"   *Mrs. B. Neilson*

Anne entered first grade last year, and soon came home telling everyone about the new math. She brought home colored blocks of graduated sizes and practiced her math with great enthusiasm. Red was twice as long as blue, orange three times as long, green four times, etc. I asked Anne what two plus three was, and she replied, "Two plus three is purple."   *Edith Clearman*

While I was working in a day-care center in Brooklyn, an alert, gay-spirited little boy who had only recently arrived in this country from Israel attached himself to me with tenacity and what I thought was love and admiration. I soon found out, however, that the child was more curious than admiring, for he had never seen a Negro before.

He trailed me doggedly, touching and "inspecting" me at every opportunity. It was during one of these inspections that this innocent four-year-old happened upon a profound truth: he touched his face, then my chocolate-brown one, and announced simply, "That's just skin."

Jewel Levias

The first day at kindergarten was drawing to a close when a little boy came up to my desk.

"Mrs. Binder, could you please tell me what we learned today?" he asked. "Because when I get home my mommy is sure to ask me."

Mrs. L. Binder

My niece's little eight-year-old came home from public school last November 10 and told her mother that she would not have any school on the following day. When asked why her reply was, "It's St. Veteran's Day." *Anne Warren*

14

My third-grader Cindy came dashing in from the school bus. "I musn't forget to take a quarter to school tomorrow!" she exclaimed excitedly.

When I asked why, she said, "Oh, it's important. Our teacher is leaving and all the kids want to give her a little momentum!"

Mrs. Roberta Rich

Dennis, our six-year-old, informed his father that he had begun hanging his cap and jacket at school in the Lost and Found Dept.

"What on earth for?" asked father.

"So I'll always know where they are," Dennis explained. *Gale Henry*

"How was your school day?" I asked our six-year-old Richard.

"Mother," he replied, "today our teacher asked me whether I had any brothers or sisters, and I told her I was an only child."

"And what did she say?" I asked.

"She said 'Thank goodness!'" he replied.

Mrs. Ritchie Smith

In a rural Nebraska school a teacher and her pupils recently spanned the long gap between "now" and "then" in agricultural history.The teacher brought an old-fashioned stone churn and two quarts of cream to school one day and staged a butter-churning session. Of the 21 pupils present—all from farm homes—not one had ever seen butter churned before. One small child watched the procedure with intense interest. Then she asked hesitantly, "Will it be butter or margarine?"

Quoted in FALLS CITY JOURNAL

Kids love to draw dinosaurs. One such artist, enthusiastic but uninformed, drew a fierce Tyrannosaurus Rex confronting a cowering spear-wielding cave man—an anachronism since old Rex was gone before man even appeared on the scene.

"What's wrong with this picture?" I asked the class.

"That's easy," said seat two, row three. "Never tease a dinosaur." *Joseph F. Hannan*

The teacher in one of our local grade schools was showing a facsimile of the Declaration of Independence to her pupils. It passed from desk to desk, and finally to Luigi, a first-generation American. The boy studied the document reverently. Then, before passing it on, he gravely added his own signature. *Katherine T. Floyd*

16

With tears in his eyes, the little boy told his kindergarten teacher that only one pair of galoshes was left in the cloakroom and they weren't his. The teacher searched under desks and in corners and could find no other galoshes. Exhausted, she asked the boy, "How can you be sure these galoshes aren't yours?"

"Mine had snow on them," the little boy replied.   *Quoted in* FAMILY WEEKLY

A teacher in primary school had been telling the class about animals. "Who can tell me what is the highest form of animal life?" she asked. A little girl bounced from her seat with the certainty of being right.

"The giraffe, ma'am," she exclaimed.

Delia Wood

The patrol has been called upon to enforce the rules of the school. On the first day, they proudly trot their first case before our enthusiastic teacher. It's a second grader, and in order to prevent his escape they have each twisted an arm behind his back. The teacher begins hearing the case.

"What did he do?" he asks.

"He got out of line," comes the answer.

"He what?"

"He got out of line in the school cafeteria. He dropped his ice cream money and went to get it."

"Well, that was all right."

"Gee, Mr. Hannan, you told us if anyone got out of line we should bring him to you."

Joseph F. Hannan

THE THINGS KIDS SAY!
Collected by Art Linkletter

One day I asked a tiny tot if he had any pets at home. "Yup!" he calmly announced. "I have a little baby porcupine that sleeps with me every night."

"Now isn't that delightful," I replied without batting an eye. "Tell us all about him." And then as quickly as a district attorney, I shot one question after another. "What's his name?"

"Porky."

"Where did you get him?"

"Downtown at a porcupine shop." He grinned up at me.

"How much did you pay for him?"

"One dollar."

"What do you feed him for lunch?"

"Lunch? Well . . . I think . . ."

"Marshmallows?" I suggested craftily.

"Yup! Marshmallows he loves." The youngster swallowed the bait.

"Aha!" I gloated. "How does he eat them?"

There was an imperceptible pause. Then with a happy smile: "He toasts them on his stickers over a campfire!"

A six year old recently assured me that someday he was going to drive an armored truck
and his Mommy and Daddy would be so proud
of him. He went on:

"It's the kind of job where you meet lots of
interesting people . . . like bank robbers. And
besides that, you make five thousand dollars a
week."

"That's a lot of money," I said. "Are you
sure you get that much?"

"Sometimes more. You just reach back in
the truck for what you want."

20

Many a strange and devastating anachronism is swallowed whole by a child determined to keep his faith in his good fairy. Take the reply of the young man who was describing a Christmas experience:

"I saw Santa Claus come right over to my bed and hang up a stocking full of presents."

"What did he look like?" I inquired curiously.

"Well, he was wearing pajama tops and carrying a bottle of beer."

Short takes:
"What do you think Politics are?"

"Another name for a horse trader."

"It's something you put in pillows."

"It's a thick book that's hard to read."

"It's kind of like a school where the teachers are real strict and there's bad boys in there."

Table manners:
"Who can think of some bad manners to watch out for?"

"Don't throw food under the table if there's not a dog under there, because it'll rot."

"You should always turn your head when you sneeze at the table, but you'd better grab your plate and take it with you, because then people can't sneak vegetables on your plate that you don't want while your head's turned."

"Don't talk with your mouth full 'cause you might choke to death."

"Never throw pies in the company's face."

"Don't use your dress for a napkin when your mother's looking."

"Ask for extra helpings instead of scraping the bottom of the plate till all the picture's worn off."

"Don't put your food in other people's drinks."

This little dreamer has a fantastic pastime:

"I like to jump on my pogo stick and bounce right up to heaven."

"What do you see there?"

"Girl angels, dog angels, cat angels and fish angels."

"No *boy* angels?" I protested.

"No. Boy angels and worm angels don't go to heaven."

CHILD PSYCHOLOGY

Overcoming my vigorous objections, my nine-year-old emerged from the store with the exact pair of shoes he said he wanted. A week later, however, the boy wistfully told me the shoes were hurting him, and that he wished he had listened to me. Exasperated, I reminded him of the tearful scene in the shoe store.

"I know," he said on the brink of tears again, "but why did you pay any attention to me? I'm only a little kid." *Mrs. Michael Holroyd*

My seven-year-old niece, Mariellen, was trying to sew a dress for her doll. Unable to thread the needle, she handed it to me and asked for help.

"Your eyes are younger than mine," I reminded her.

"Yes," Mariellen agreed, "but you have older fingers." *Mrs. Emil S. Holicek*

I was deeply engrossed in conversation with a visiting friend. Apparently my little Wendy felt that she wasn't getting her usual attention for she suddenly said, "Would anyone like to be smiled at?" *Mrs. David Gordon*

My young brother was showing a neighbor's child through our house for the first time, and I heard him announce proudly as they passed the bar: "And this is my father's chemistry set."   *Victoria B. Garcia*

A minister in a town in Alberta is used to having his tiny daughter hustle up from Sunday school to help him shake hands with the congregation on the way out of church. He was a bit taken aback one recent Sunday, however, to notice that his eldest son had also joined the line and was busily collecting from customers on his paper route whom he had missed the day before on his regular rounds.

Quoted in MACLEAN'S MAGAZINE

While we were visiting our neighbors, their frisky new puppy started to lick our three-year-old son Gary's hand, frightening the boy who started to cry. To soothe Gary, my husband told him that the puppy wasn't trying to bite him; he just wanted to play.

Helpfully our five-year-old daughter Julie piped up, "The puppy was just tasting you, Gary, to see if you're good enough to eat." Our laughter luckily dispelled Gary's fears.

Mrs. Gary L. Crugher

A young mother had taken her five-year-old to an amusement park for the day. Along toward mid-afternoon her feet began to give out, and she decided to sit down for an hour or so. "Here's a dollar for you," she told the child. "Now tell me how you are going to spend it."

"Well," replied the happy youngster, "I'll get an ice-cream cone, a candied apple, some peanuts, popcorn—" Catching an ominous expression in her mother's eye, she broke off, then added quickly, "And a green vegetable, of course."

Quoted in THE PRESIDIO

My six-year-old son, Larry had gone to the dentist and was quite surprised to learn that he had several new cavities instead of just the one he knew about.

"It must be because of your sweet tooth," I told him after we'd come home.

"Why don't we have the dentist pull it the next time?" Larry suggested. "Then the others will be all right." *Roberta Rich*

One morning I looked into the nursery and found my six-year-old son laboriously putting a bandage on his thumb.

"What happened?" I cried, afraid he was really injured.

"I hit it with a hammer," said the boy.

"You poor darling," I sympathized. "But why didn't I hear you cry?"

"I didn't think I had to cry," he explained, "because I thought you were out."

Mrs. Thomas Gray

As the father of six children, I used to think I was ready for anything—especially when I came home from work each afternoon. Then one day my youngest son, Jimmy, confronted me on the front porch.

"Hi, Dad," he said with a twinkle in his

eye. "Glad to see you smiling. Just keep smiling, Dad, while I tell you how I broke the kitchen window this morning!" *James Everett*

The piano teacher was expected any minute, and my son, Tommy, was preparing to take his lesson.

"Did you wash your hands?" I inquired as usual.

"Yes."

"And your face?"

"Yes, Mother."

"And did you wash behind your ears?"

"On her side, I did, Mother!"

Mrs. Arthur McBride

When my five-year-old son came to the table with his hands very dirty, I told him he must go wash and not come back until they were clean.

After a good deal of time had passed, I called, "Billy, how are your hands—are they clean yet?"

"Not clean," he replied. "But I got them to match?" *Caroline Becker*

During an American history lesson I was citing George Washington for his honesty, bravery, sincerity, perseverence, kindness and initiative. I then asked the class for what position they thought a man with all these qualities would best be suited.

There followed a long period of deep silence. Finally one little girl put up her hand and said, "I think he would make a very nice husband!"   *Dorothea Kent*

It was a lovely October day, and the leaves around our house were a gorgeous red and gold. I had promised to take my four-year-old granddaughter for a walk along the creek. But my cooking and other household chores kept me busy inside.

The little girl waited for a long time patiently. Then she took my hand and pulled me along.

"Stop working, Grandma," she said. "Let's go outside and get some use out of the world."
                                            Mrs. Archie McKee

IT'S A LITTLE WORLD

Our little girl likes horror movies and space-age monsters, and she loves to dream up her own versions to scare her young friends. One afternoon I found her making strange faces in front of a mirror. Closer examination revealed that the youngster was crying.

"What on earth is wrong, dear?" I asked.

"Oh, I wish I didn't have this dimple in my cheek," she responded. "Because when I want to look like a vampire, it spoils the effect!"

Jean Bonner

As I was doing my housework one day, I heard my six-year-old son telling his playmate about his mean little brother.

"The only reason he's here now is because the stork couldn't stand him any longer."

Mrs. James Shaw

Note left by a ten-year-old boy for his mother, who was shopping when he got home from school: "I have a very bad headache and a stomach ache. I have taken two aspirins and a glass of milk and gone out to play baseball."

Quoted in DENVER POST

A group of small girls was taken to visit the Museum of Science and Industry in Chicago. When they came to the project showing the stages of development of the human embryo, they stood in awe before the first exhibit. Then a bright young miss dashed down to the final one, ran back and announced, "It's a boy!"

Margaret H. Campbell

From a child's letter to her Congressman: "I am making up a new Moonian language for speaking when we get on the moon. I will let you have some of the words. Just say what you want these words to mean. Ragoolig. Qmalf. Jaalapoomwah. Cish. Let me know what you think."

Quoted in THE CHRISTIAN SCIENCE MONITOR

The garden was at its peak of production, and, like the proverbial ant, I was busily putting some of its fruits away for the winter. As I opened the freezer to deposit a batch, I noticed a row of what seemed to be empty plastic freezer cartons. On examination, I found that each contained a fly, frozen stiff.

I was removing the cartons and puzzling over them when my eight-year-old grandson bounded in. Seeing what I was doing, he said,

"Oh, Grandma, don't take those out of the freezer. Those are TV dinners for my turtle!"
Anne Schiber

Several starched and becurled little girls and slicked-up little boys were lined up on the platform waiting turns to play in a piano recital. The name of one little girl was called, but no child stepped forward. There was an uncomfortable silence which was finally broken by a small voice saying, "Mom! I can't get the chewing gum off my fingers!" *Dorothea Kent*

In Atlanta, one member of a Halloween group hung back as the others collected their candy, then said, "You don't have to give me any candy, but I sure would like to use your bathroom." *Quoted in* ATLANTA CONSTITUTION

The Little Leaguer put all his 60 pounds into a ferocious swing and connected—barely. The ball, scraped by the bottom of the bat, jiggled straight back to the pitcher, who groped and fumbled a moment. There was still plenty of time to nail the batter at first, but the pitcher's throw soared high over the first baseman's head. The slugger flew on toward second. Somebody retrieved the ball. The next throw sailed into left field. The hitter swaggered into third, puffing through a man-sized grin. "Oh, boy!" he said. "That's the first triple I ever hit in my whole life."

Quoted in DES MOINES TRIBUNE

The other day, hearing my five-year-old scream at the top of his lungs, I ran into the play room and found the baby pulling his hair.

"Don't cry," I comforted my son, "little sister doesn't understand that it hurts you."

I returned to my work. A few minutes later more shrieks sent me running back.

"What's the baby crying about?" I demanded.

"She knows how it feels to have her hair pulled," my son replied.   *Mrs. Edna Bowman*

A five-year-old Memphis girl, with a real feeling for tradition, named the bunny she got for Easter "Rabbit E. Lee."

Quoted in ASSOCIATED PRESS

A man who lives in the suburbs of Los Angeles and works in the advertising department of a large metropolitan newspaper had never been able to figure out the deferential attitude, bordering on awe, of the children on his block.

Out for a stroll recently, he came upon a group of little boys discussing the newest American satellite hurtling through space. He paused to say hello to the youngsters, and suddenly everything became clear. One of the boys asked, "Are you *really* a space salesman?"

Quoted in the WALL STREET JOURNAL

Schoolgirls in Bockenheim, a suburb of Frankfurt, Germany, sent out invitations to a class party reading: "Everyone who doesn't bring a boy has to bring two soft drinks."

Quoted in MILWAUKEE JOURNAL

My six-year-old son was down in the dumps after losing a tooth. He looked enviously at his fourteen-year-old brother, who wore braces, and said, "At least you'll never lose your teeth —they're chained in."   *Mrs. Gary Hunter*

My eight-year-old girl came home from school to announce that she planned to marry a school-mate.

"That's fine. Does he have a job?" I asked.

"Oh yes," my daughter replied. "He erases the blackboard."   *Mrs. W. C. Warner*

As I walked into the kitchen one morning, I overheard my small son talking to a friend about his baby sister. "She has some teeth, but her words haven't come in yet."

Mrs. Robert Cannon

A young mother was about to leave her house wearing a miniskirt, fishnet stockings, poor-boy sweater, plastic earrings and white lip-stick. At the door her little daughter looked her over, then exclaimed, "Mommy, you look like a dead teenager!"   *Emily Watkins*

LETTERS FROM CAMP
Collected by Bill Adler

Dear Mom and Dad,
Monday we played baseball.
Tuesday we went rowing.
Wednesday we went on a hike.
Thursday we had a campfire.
Friday we played tennis.
Saturday we played basketball.
Sunday we played volleyball.
I am bored. There is nothing to do up here.

Your son, Fred

Dear Mom and Dad,
I cannot lie to you. I am not fine. I have 103 degree temperature and I broke my leg. But don't worry. At least I didn't get Chicken Pox like the other kids in my bunk.

Your son, Norman

Dear Folks,
One of the boys broke his leg. They had a big fire in the recreation hall. My counselor had his appendix out. The boy in the bed next to me almost drowned. The water pipe broke in the kitchen and they had a flood. A tree fell

down when the lightning hit it and they found a big rat in one of the bunks. Nothing else is new.   Love, Peter

Dear Mom and Dad,

   I like the desserts here. Today for lunch I had apple pie, jello, chocolate pudding, and ice cream. What did you eat today?   Love, Billy

Dear Mom and Dad,

   I have written a poem about our counselor.
      Spaghetti on meat balls
      Ice cream on cake,
      Our counselor should drown in the lake.
                                    Love, Roger

One Week's Letters from the Same Boy
Monday: Today we played baseball and I got three hits. I like this camp.
Tuesday: We played baseball and I hit a home run. I want to come back here again next year.
Wednesday: I hit a double and a triple in the baseball game. This is the best camp I have ever been at.
Thursday: I made a double play in the baseball game. It's terrific up here.
Friday: I struck out four times in the baseball game. I hate it up here. I want to come home.

Dear Mom,

Here is a picture they took of all the boys in the bunk. I am the one with his arm in the sling.   Jeff

Dear Mom and Dad,

Guess what? The doctor says I have athlete's feet. I guess I really am a good baseball player.
                                    Love, Dan

Dear Mom and Dad,

Every time we brush our teeth right we get a point. I owe six points.   Love, Barbara

Same Girl Three Weeks in a Row

1st Week

Dear Mother,

I met a wonderful boy at the dance and someday I'm going to marry him.

2nd Week

Dear Mother,

I met a new boy at the dance who I am going to marry. I really mean it.

3rd Week

Dear Mother,

I met a boy at the dance this Saturday who is wonderful. I'm going to marry him for sure.

Dear Folks,

We are having a good time. We made up a poem about the camp.

Butter goes to bread

Hammer goes to nail

A comb goes to your head

and

This place is like a jail.   Love, Sheldon

THE GOSPEL ACCORDING TO
DICK AND JANE

One evening my three small children and I were seated around the dinner table discussing the nature of God—that guardian of children who always knows what is happening. Interested, my youngest daughter asked me,

"Mama—how does God hear everything we say?"

To which my five-year-old son replied in all seriousness, "Cause He's got big ears, that's how."   *Cheryl Asbury*

When my sister and her little girl came to visit me one day, I showed them some artificial flowers I had made from crepe paper. "That's what I call real roses, even if I made them myself," I proudly said.

My little niece looked up at me and said, "Won't God be surprised when He finds out about it?"   *Mrs. Ann Sokol*

Our young daughter, Alice, had recently learned the Ten Commandments. I was thus rather surprised when I found the cookie jar that had been full in the morning half empty by afternoon. I called Alice into the kitchen and said: "I think the cookie jar must know all about the Ten Commandments because it has heard us going over them many times. Now, suppose that the cookie jar could talk. Which Commandment would the cookie jar say had been broken?"

I expected the answer to be, "Thou shalt not steal," or "Honor thy father and mother."

However, Alice thought carefully for a moment, and then answered, "I think the cookie jar would say, 'Let the little children come unto me.' "

Rev. David Johnson in WALLACE'S FARMER

One afternoon my little boy, who has long, straight blond hair, was watching me comb his sister's very curly locks.

"Mommy," he asked, "why didn't God plow furrows in my hair like He did in Janie's?"

Jean Bonner

It was our first visit to New York City—and for my son, the first time he had ridden on an elevator. We were going to the top of the Empire State Building. As we shot past the sixty-fifth floor, he gulped, turned to me and said, "Daddy, does God know we're coming?"

Glenn Meade

One morning in Sunday School I was leading a lesson concerning Lot's wife. "Do you know why she turned into a pillar of salt?" I asked.

There was silence. Then a youngster who seldom said anything raised his hand.

"Yes?" I asked.

"I know why my mother turned into a tree," he said.

Mystified, I asked the boy to explain.

"Well," he said, "my dad was trying to teach her to drive, and . . ." *David Crowder*

I watched my four-year-old playing happily alone in the back yard, throwing his ball in the air and running after it.

"Having lots of fun?" I asked.

"Yep! We're having real fun."

"We?" I questioned. "Who are you with?"

"God," he answered. "I throw the ball up and God throws it down."

Mary Ann Velasquez

Caught in church, while conducting himself with considerably less than angelic behavior, the five-year-old brother of a friend of mine was given a thorough shaking and scolding by one of the nuns in attendance.

Later, asked by his mother what he had done to bring about the reprimand, the youngster explained: "Nothing. I was just talking to Tommy—and that's when Mrs. God sneaked up and shook me quiet." *Janice Jost*

From the time Susy was old enough to talk, my husband and I began some simple religious training at home. When she turned five, we felt she was ready for her first visit to Sunday School in "God's House."

That Sunday morning, Susy took an unusually long time to dress, explaining, "So God will know I want to look nice for Him." She was excited on the way to church, but when we walked up to the door her eagerness turned to dismay.

"Mommy!" Susy cried, "God doesn't know we're here!" "Why yes He does, dear," I assured her. "No He doesn't," she insisted. "He's not looking out the window."

Jean Bonner

Father was worried with bundles and burdens. Mother's nerve reached the breaking point more than once. The little girl seemed to be in the way wherever she went. Finally, she was hustled up to bed. As she knelt to pray, the feverish excitement so mixed her up that she said, "Forgive us our Christmases, as we forgive those who Christmas against us."

Leslie B. Flynn

A young Catholic priest drove a bus to pick up children of migrant workers and bring them to school during the summer.

A seven-year-old boy didn't want to go to school one day. The priest kept insisting that the lad should get all the schooling he could so that someday he would have a good job.

Looking up at the priest, the boy asked,

"How long did you go to school?"

After the priest told him the number of years, the boy retorted, "And you're only a bus driver!"   *Mrs. Evelyn Stannard*

Little Patty Lamm, the seven-year-old daughter of a Cleveland publicist, was painting something when her father walked in and asked what it was. She said, "I'm painting a picture of God."

"Darling," said Pop, "it's very sweet of you, but nobody ever saw God and nobody knows what He looks like."

"Well," said the little doll, "*now* they'll know."   *Joey Adams*

Two youngsters were walking home from Sunday School after having been taught a lesson on the devil. One little boy was overheard saying to the other, "What do you think about all this devil business?"

The other youngster replied thoughtfully, "Well, you know how Santa Claus turned out. It's probably just our dad."

Quoted in Columbus, Wisconsin,
JOURNAL-REPUBLICAN

IT'S A BIG WORLD

Several people in our neighborhood recently spent a hectic afternoon trying to restore a little lost youngster to his mother. Every woman in the room began to cry, too, when the mother tearfully hugged her boy. We had all thought he was too young to talk—but he wasn't. He told his mother, "I already cried. You don't have to."   *Frances Turner*

The hour was early, but already several of the Oregon campsites were bustling with activity. I was washing up at one of the comfort stations when I noticed a youngster awaiting her turn. Remarking that she was up early, I told her that my lazy boys wouldn't get out of their sleeping bags. "Well," she confided, "my Daddy always tries to sleep late, but Mommie knows how to get him up."

Unable to resist the bait, I asked, "What does your Mommie do?"

"Oh," she said, "she just pulls the plug on his air mattress."   *Mrs. J. Michael Vukich*

I was tinkering again with the power-mower when my little boy ran up and exclaimed:

"Wow! you should see the great new lawn-mower the people next door got—it doesn't need gas or anything. All you have to do is push it!" *Joseph Turowski*

Five-year-old Timmy and I were watching a rough, bone-crunching football game on television. After a while Timmy asked, "Dad—what position did you play in college?"

"I played in the backfield and carried the ball," I replied.

Timmy watched the game for a while longer, and then said, "When I get big and go to college I know what position I want to play."

"The same as I did?" I asked hopefully.

"No," Timmy said. "I want to play the position that the man in the black and white shirt with the whistle plays." *Norm Edmonds*

A boy was overheard saying to a friend as they left a movie: "I like television a lot better. It's not so far to the bathroom."

Quoted in CORONET

My four-year-old sister went to my mother at work in the kitchen, looked up at her adoringly and exclaimed, "Mother, I like you better than any other leading brand!" *Kerry Klein*

Our son Fred had just come home after a school trip through the museum of natural history. When we asked where his teacher had taken him that day, he turned up his nose and said: "Oh, we went to see a dead circus!"

Mrs. John Rockwell

A little boy deposited two overdue books on the desk of a public library and handed his past-due letter, plus the eighteen cent fine it called for, to the clerk.

Then he asked, "Please can I have the letter back? It's the first one I ever got!"

Quoted in LAUGH DAY (*Bennet Cerf*)

Mrs. Ann Brewer turned on her radio to hear the Presidential inauguration ceremonies in Washington and the first voice was of a clergyman.

"What's he saying?" asked her five-year-old son, Clark.

"He's praying," said Mrs. Brewer. "He's talking to God."

Then came the well-known resonant voice of Senator Everett M. Dirkson, who acted as the director of ceremonies.

"Is that God answering?" asked Clark.

Quoted in ASSOCIATED PRESS

I was carrying my two-year-old up the subway escalator when he turned his little head and cried out, "The stairs are following us, Mommie—look!" *Mrs. Albert Long*

When our neighbor's little girl answered the phone, she told the caller that her mother was not available, but that she could take a message. The caller asked that her mother telephone Capitol 5-6428 as soon as possible. After a long silence, the puzzled little girl ventured, "Please, could you tell me how to make a capital 5?" *Veronica C. Drake*

We were visiting New York City and decided to take our young son to see a musical. I began to feel a little uneasy when the chorus girls appeared, clad only in scanty green and white ribbons.

As the number ended, my son leaned over and said, "Mom, did you see that?"

"See what?" I asked apprehensively.

"Those girls are wearing our school colors."

Mrs. Nelson Ashly

At nightfall recently our four-year-old son Dave was helping me with the farm chores. On the way back to the house, he looked uneasily at the darkened sky, and not willing to admit he was afraid, he said, "You can carry my hand if you want to, Mama."

Mrs. Ken Buckingham

When I took my daughter's youngest child to the circus for the first time, her eyes grew wide with awe as she watched the tightrope walker perform.

"Isn't it exciting to see that lady run across that little wire?" I asked.

"Oh," she gasped, "There's a wire? I thought she was walking on air."

Mrs. H. Priday

An ear infection caused our young son to go to the doctor who used a large metal syringe to wash out the ear. When he had finished, our boy jumped off the table and excitedly exclaimed,

"Wow, wait till I tell the kids I was brainwashed!"
Mrs. Peter Laudis

A Father's Day composition written by an eight-year-old: "He can climb the highest mountain or swim the biggest ocean. He can fly the fastest plane and fight the strongest tiger. My father can do anything. But most of the time he just throws out the garbage."

Quoted in BOYS ARE VERY
FUNNY PEOPLE (*Bill Adler*)

Four-year-old Michael had whined and begged to go on a hike with his Cub-Scout brother. Finally, his frustrated mother agreed.

As she accompanied them to the door, however, Michael paused and asked plaintively, "Mommy, could Daddy drive us on our hike?"
Mrs. Charles Healey

A sixth-grade girl, assigned to write her autobiography, included in her paper: "I have a brother 13 years old. He plays on the school football team and is an offensive throwback."

Muriel Mallon

Eight-year-old's essay on "What a mom means to a kid": "A mother is a person who takes care of her kids and gets their meals and if she's not there when you get home from school, you wouldn't know how to get your dinner and you wouldn't feel like eating it anyhow."

Quoted in EXECUTIVES DIGEST

My son Bub was a fourth-grader when he bounced in from school one day and asked, "Mama, what is sex?"

I launched into a stammering, rather clinical dissertation on the facts of life. Bub looked more and more puzzled as I talked. Finally he pulled out the identification card from his new wallet and said, "But, Mama, I'll never get all that stuff in this little space under 'Sex'!"

Mrs. Wiley B. Van Wagner

Some youngsters at summer camp write very little but say a great deal. For instance, a 10-year-old New York lad wrote his parents from Vermont: "This camp has everything and they don't need me."

Quoted in NEW YORK WORLD-TELEGRAM

One father of a dozen children admits to a little difficulty keeping track of them. Take the night when the telephone rang after the family was asleep. Father answered the phone and heard a request for John. He called upstairs and heard a growing hubbub as young voices relayed the request from room to room. Father got a little impatient. "I don't want a riot. Just tell John to come down and answer the phone!" he shouted.

Finally a tiny voice penetrated the noise: "John is married. He doesn't live here anymore." *Quoted in* SEATTLE TIMES

DOCTOR, LAWYER, MERCHANT, CHIEF

Collected by Art Linkletter

Occupational hazards:

"What's your amibition?"

"To be a skin diver in the Navy."

"What if you saw a man-eating shark?"

"I'd tell him, 'Go find a man, I'm just a little boy.'"

"What will you be some day, Sharon?"

"A movie star."

"I'll give you an acting job: Say 'Arthur!' like you're angry."

"Arthur! Like you're angry!"

"So you want to be a nurse. What if I came in with a stomach ache?"

"I'd give you a shot."

"What if I had smallpox?"

"I'd give you a shot."

"What if I had chickenpox?"

"Another shot."

"What if I just had a runny nose?"

"I'd wipe it."

There was more truth than comedy in the words of one young man who wanted to be a general in our Air Force.

I asked him what's the most important thing an Air Force general has to do, and he told me:

"Be sure you are fighting the right war."

"What's your ambition?"

"To be a fireman."

"What if you saw a big fat lady in a tall building yelling for help?"

"I'd send her a big fat fireman."

"So you want to be a fireman. What's the hardest thing a fireman does?"

"Puts out fires."

"That's right. What's the easiest thing a fireman does?"

"Plays poker all day at the station."

"How do you know that?"

"My dad's a fireman."

"What do you want to be?"

"A nurse."

"What's the most important thing to remember?"

"To smile and tell everybody they have to wait an hour."

"What do you want to be, Donald?"

"An artist so I can draw rainbows."

"What's at the end of the rainbow?"

"A plug."

"Where have you been seeing your rainbows?"

"In the bathtub."

"What do you want to be?"

"A policeman."

"What's the most important thing to remember?"

"Don't wet your bed."

"Would you like to be President?"

"Not me!"

"Why not?"

"Because no matter what happens, it's all your fault!"

"What do you want to be?"

"A lifeguard."

"Suppose you saw a man drowning. What would you do first?"

"Build a raft."

"What do you want to be?"

"A woodchopper, because I love to see those great big trees come falling down in the forest."

"What do you yell when a big tree starts to fall?"

"Help!"

"What do you want to be?"

"A mother with three children."

"What kind of husband do you want?"

"I don't want one."

"What would you like to be?"

"A ballerina with a fluffy skirt."

"What's the hardest thing a ballerina does?"

"Zip up the back of her dress."

LOGIC À LA SMALL FRY

The lesson in natural history had been about the rhinoceros, and I was following it with an oral test.

"Now, name something," I said, "that is very dangerous to get near to, and that has horns."

"I know, Miss Lane, I know!" called little Jennie.

"Well, Jennie, what is it?" I asked.

"An automobile!" Jennie replied triumphantly.   *Rita Lane*

I was reading a poem to the class about Columbus. As I went along, I encouraged participation by asking questions about the poem. At one point I said, "Do you know why Columbus called the strange men he met in the New World 'Indians'?"

In the back of the room a little girl raised her hand. When called upon, she said, "Because he thought he was in Indiana!"

Jane Patrick

Six-year-old Terry was fascinated by stories about ants that I'd read to him from a book he received for Christmas. He was especially interested in how hard ants worked.

Not long after, he and a friend were watching some ants crawl out of a hole. As his friend started to step on one of them, my son shouted, "Don't kill him! He's only trying to make a living!"   *Mrs. Marjorie A. Farley*

One evening at dinner we were discussing good manners, and I brought up the subject of finger-bowls. I explained that they were small bowls filled with scented water in which you dipped your fingers to wash them, and that fingerbowls were used in restaurants and at formal dinners.

Our son, Johnny, considered the explanation a moment and then said, "Boy — their manners must be a lot worse than mine if they have to wash their hands while they eat!"

David B. Kane

Michael brought my attention to some mischief his brothers were up to at some distance away.

"How come you see so far away, when I can hardly see them?" I asked.

"That's easy," said Michael. "I got long eyes."   *Mrs. B. Konkel*

58

Among many birthday gifts, our neighbor's five-year-old received a toy watch. When I asked her, "Is that a real watch, Barby?" she answered without a moment's hesitation:

"Yes, but it doesn't work real."

Mrs. Richard Aylward

My neighbor dropped in while my five-year-old niece was visiting me.

"Where did you get such beautiful, big, blue eyes?" she asked my small niece.

"I don't know," the child answered. "They just came with my face."

Mrs. Pearl B. Marcus

One cool summer evening a neighbor's five-year-old girl came to visit. When I asked her where her shoes were, she replied, "I never wear shoes when I go barefoot."

Mrs. Russell Niehaus

My neighbor reported that my six-year-old son was watching her dampen clothes for ironing and asked her what she was doing.

"I'm sprinkling clothes," she told him. "Doesn't your mother do this?"

He unhesitatingly replied, "Oh no, she washes them." *Mrs. Harold Warmbe*

Shortly after we moved into a new neighborhood our six-year-old was invited to join a "Cookie Club." The only requirement was to furnish cookies at the first meeting. When I asked our daughter's new friend how often the club met, she replied, "Oh, we just meet when we have a new member."

Mrs. W. M. Ayers

A parochial-school girl went to confession Saturday and came home annoyed because she had had to wait so long. "That church ought to get more efficient," she told her mother. "They should have a fast line for people with six sins or less." *Quoted in* CHICAGO TRIBUNE

Little Mark's mother found a big wad of grass in one of the pockets of his jeans as she was doing the washing.

She asked Mark if he was collecting grass these days.

"No," he replied, "not me. But that worm had to have something to eat, didn't he?"

Dorothea Kent

It took my four-year-old to broaden my knowledge of anatomy when she reneged on dressing herself the other day. She supported her argument, observing, "The buttons are behind and I'm in front." *Mrs. M. W. Johnstone*

Asked why he got so dirty, one little boy told his mother, "Well, I'm a lot closer to the ground then you are."

Quoted in FARM JOURNAL

Set in Monotype Walbaum, a light, open typeface
designed by Justus Erich Walbaum (1768-1839),
who was a type founder at Goslar and at Weimar.
Printed on Hallmark Eggshell Book paper.
Designed by Harald Peter.